PRINTABLE BUSINESS

LEARN HOW TO BUILD AND GROW A SUCCESSFUL BUSINESS ON ETSY OR YOUR OWN STOREFRONT!

Copyright © All rights reserved worldwide.

YOUR RIGHTS: This book is restricted to your personal use only. It does not come with any other rights.

LEGAL DISCLAIMER: This book is protected by international copyright law and may not be copied, reproduced, given away, or used to create derivative works without the publisher's expressed permission. The publisher retains full copyrights to this book.

The author has made every reasonable effort to be as accurate and complete as possible in the creation of this book and to ensure that the information provided is free from errors; however, the author/publisher/ reseller assumes no responsibility for errors, omissions, or contrary interpretation of the subject matter herein and does not warrant or represent at any time that the contents within are accurate due to the rapidly changing nature of the internet.

Any perceived slights of specific persons, peoples, or organizations are unintentional.

The purpose of this book is to educate, and there are no guarantees of income, sales, or results implied. The publisher/author/reseller can, therefore, not be held accountable for any poor results you may attain when implementing the techniques or when following any guidelines set out for you in this book.

Any product, website, and company names mentioned in this report are the trademarks or copyright properties of their respective owners. The author/publisher/reseller are not associated or affiliated with them in any way. Nor does the referred product, website, and company names sponsor, endorse, or approve this product.

COMPENSATION DISCLOSURE: Unless otherwise expressly stated, you should assume that the links contained in this book may be affiliate links, and either the author/publisher/reseller will earn a commission if you click on them and buy the product/service mentioned in this book. However, the author/publisher/reseller disclaims any liability that may result from your involvement with any such websites/products. You should perform due diligence before buying the mentioned products or services.

This constitutes the entire license agreement. Any disputes or terms not discussed in this agreement are at the sole discretion of the publisher.

Table of Contents

Introduction

If you're looking for a profitable side hustle that could easily turn into a full-time income, selling printables online is one of the **easiest ways to get started**.

Across all markets, printables are in demand. To funnel traffic to websites, content pages, squeeze pages and even as training elements, people use them.

These printables provide an simple way to get organized, set goals and keep on track, so naturally, regardless of the industry in which you are involved, they are always in demand.

In other words, **Printables sell a dream of a better life:** they represent organized, creative and successful people.

They're designed to help people improve the quality of their lives in some way. **They offer a workable system to organizing the chaos.**

Fortunately, in order to make lovely printables that people would enjoy, you don't have to go through a lengthy learning curve.

By simply outsourcing the designs and templates to freelance markets such as Upwork.com, you can easily avoid the repetitive design process and steep learning curve.

Hot Tip: You can find done-for-you printable design packs that come with source files (for easy editing) as well as commercial-use rights on design sites like https://shop.nicheraiders.com

These printable design reseller packs will save you a lot of time by entirely eliminating the work involved in printable design!

There are many different ways you can set up a printable business in a matter of a few days.

Then, you can easily jumpstart sales by sending targeted traffic to your new shop or website using the power of social media, particularly Pinterest.

I'll show you how to do all of this and more within this special report, so strap yourself in and get ready for a no-fluff guide to making money in the incredibly profitable (and evergreen!) world of printables.

Let's begin!

Setting up Shop

There are many ways to create an online shop so you can start selling your downloadable products, but one of the easiest ways to get started is with Etsy, available at https://www.Etsy.com

There are just a handful of explanations here:
With an Etsy store, since you are in direct touch with your client base, you can easily create a mailing list of customers and increase your sales more efficiently and easily than ever before.

In addition, since you will be able to grow a tribe of customers and create a brand you are in full charge of, you will never be reliant on only one marketplace.

There'll be no guesswork.

You'll know where your buyers come from, what they're interested in and how to create additional products they'll want to buy. And making money online will never be easier once you've built that community of your own.

Plus , people are already on Etsy looking for printables! This ensures that you will be able to quickly tap into an ever-growing marketplace-active consumer base.

So even if you don't launch your own marketing campaigns, chances are you're going to be able to start generating revenue from current traffic from Etsy. Uh, quick!

And finally, there are valuable tools that make it easy to create Etsy listings that stand out from the crowd. I'm talking about resources like https://www.MarmaLead.com that not only break down your existing Etsy listings to show you how to improve your outreach, but they grade your listings based on focus keywords, exposure and more!

You may want to choose a shop name carefully when it comes to building an Etsy shop, and customize your storefront so that it clearly reflects your brand.

This includes a high-quality store banner, a distinctive logo and summary of the store / tagline, and in-demand printable items, of course.

Let's get started:

Step 1: Create your Etsy Account:

Head on over to https://Etsy.com and create your account.

Make sure to fill in all the profile and account areas, including your payment information, address and add a credit card to your account so that Etsy can charge you for each listing whenever it needs to be renewed.

Including store language, country and currency, you may also want to configure your shop preferences.

Next, make sure to set the name of your shop so that it is exactly the same name as your blog (if you are planning to build one, and I recommend that you do!). The key is to be coherent on all platforms.

Your shop name should be between 4-20 characters, and no spaces or special characters should be used.

Whatever shop name you assign will also become your Etsy web address and will look something like this: keyword.etsy.com

Step 2: Add Your First Product

The next step will be to stock your shop with at least one printable product.

Note that you can't create an Etsy shop without having at least one available product, so if you have yet to create your first printable offer, you'll want to do that first and then return to your Etsy account to complete the process.

Each product listing can include up to 10 images and you'll want to use every available space.

However, you don't need to have all 10-graphics ready. When adding your first product listing, you can always start by just adding one image and then go back in and add additional images later.

Step 3: Complete Your Payment Settings

Set your payment preferences, including how you wish to be paid (Paypal, check or money order, etc.)

Then, set up billing. You'll need to add a credit card to your account.

Step 4: Create your Brand Graphics

Now that you have a brand-new Etsy account, it's time to customize your shop! The important thing is to make sure all your images look alike while highlighting the different products.

You want a cohesive, unforgettable brand to be created. We all use a fixed color scheme, and they stick to it, if you look at the top printable sellers on Etsy.

Not only does it look more professional, it makes people begin to understand your name, so they know who you are and what you have to sell when they see your pins or visit your blog. Creating your shop graphics doesn't have to be difficult or time consuming. My personal "trick" is to create one set of templates using a resource like https://www.Canva.com and then re-use them over and over again, simply replacing the product snapshots with ones that represent the current product offered.

Note: It's always best to create printables based on **evergreen,**

time-tested markets, and then figure out a way to put **your own unique twist** on each product.

That way, you're offering something fresh and new, while still sticking within those popular, established niches that are continuing to grow.

Launching Your Shop

There are a few things you'll want to do when it comes to optimizing your sales to give your shop an immediate increase in visibility.

You may want to focus on building up the inventory to begin with. I always suggest that you set your initial product goal to be at least 50 printable items.

Yeah, it'll take time to do this, but it'll be worth it! The more products, the better because it will help you rank for various keywords / focus terms that maximize revenue.

After you create your shop, you'll want to add categories for your products. This will help you rank for the keywords used in category titles, but more importantly, it helps shoppers navigate your store.

Note: I recommend starting off with only 3-4 categories until you build up your inventory. You don't want any of your categories to be empty or to inundate your customers with too many options.

Categories help to organize the store easier and help potential clients easily find what they are most interested in, so keep them targeted. Use simple keywords like: Student Planners, Goals & Productivity , Health & Fitness or Company Planners as examples to do this.

There are a couple of different areas that you may want to optimize when it comes to optimizing your Etsy store.

Tags:

You use tags **everywhere**, not just in the keyword boxes associated with each product listing, but in your titles as well.

Etsy gives you the opportunity to include 13 tags that describe your product and you'll want to use all 13 of these so you can increase your chances at being matched to a search.

Titles:

A well-crafted title that triggers the Etsy search engine to show your listing will naturally drive in sales, but one thing you need to know is that your tags and titles should be the **EXACT SAME.**

You won't increase your ranking by using different keywords in your title and tags. In fact, using the same keywords is a critical step in fully optimizing your listing so you're more easily found.

Here are a few other things to keep in mind:

- Etsy allows up to 140 characters in your title. While many people recommend using up every bit of spacing, from my own research and stats, shorter titles often convert better.

- Shorter titles are easier for a buyer to read and understand. And if you construct it so that your title is very clear and direct, you'll be able to cut out a lot of words that aren't necessary, nor helpful in boosting visibility.

- Etsy uses your title to determine which keywords you'll appear/rank for when someone enters a search phrase on Etsy. Therefore, it's important that you include some of your best keywords in your title, while also keeping it short and to the point.

The Power of Keywords

It all starts with the keywords you use inside your product descriptions and titles as well as how thoroughly you have optimized your storefront when it comes to optimizing your Etsy shop so that you can drive targeted traffic to your listings.

Learning how to properly research and use focus keywords in your product pages will not only help you optimize your listings and overall shop, but you'll begin to see what's selling based on **actual search volume.**

Meaning, you'll get hard data that you can work with. No guesswork. You'll know what people are actively searching for and buying so you can create those types of products for your own shop.

To start, you'll want to focus on just a **single keyword** that you know you'll be able to rank for. We call this our **focus keyword**.

This keyword is the primary one for which you expect to rank in a listing of items. In all areas of your product page, you emphasize this keyword while using secondary keywords to fill in the gaps.

Your keyword for emphasis should always appear in the title and description of the product. The other keywords, or secondary keywords, are known as supporting keywords.

The key is to choose the best focus keywords possible that are relevant to your product and will directly target the right audience.

Time Saver Tip: I always encourage people to invest in an Etsy-specific research tool such as https://www.MarmaLead.com, rather than a generic, all-encompassing SEO product that isn't designed specifically for Etsy because they know the way Etsy works!

MarmaLead was responsible for knocking out stores that were not recognizable and converting them into top-selling superstars.

There are other ways to build your focus keyword lists easily, beginning with Etsy itself, if you want to go it alone and do the job yourself.

Start by searching the market for items and then visit 15-20 different shops. Scroll to the bottom of these product pages and you can find keywords that are used by such product pages. Write these down and then run them to assess the search volume by Google Keywords.

Google & Amazon

You can use Google's search bar as well as Amazon's and let auto-complete help you identify commonly-used keyword strings.

Start by typing in a few keywords for the seed and then see what comes up. Also, to see other common keyword phrases used by on-site users, make sure you scroll to the bottom of the first search results page of every Google search.

The same auto-suggestion feature is also provided by Amazon. Take it a step further with Amazon, and check out some of the book pages in your niche for journals and planners. Any low-content book could be transformed into a printable kit, so that your Etsy listings can conveniently use the keywords you find on the product pages.

Pay attention to keywords used in the product titles as well as the bullet-points used on planner and journal pages. You'll quickly find a ton of relevant keywords that you can add to your seed keyword list!

Pinterest: http://www.Pinterest.com
A favorite hot spot for keywords based on popular tags.

You can start by entering in your primary keyword phrase and see where it takes you, but the better way is by browsing the categories.

Google Trends

If you want to be notified of when certain search terms are used so you can figure out how popular a keyword phrase is, hop on over to https://trends.google.com/trends

To see what pops up, start by typing in a keyword term, such as "pregnancy printable."

You will also be able to see similar search queries, which is a perfect way to find widely used keyword strings that can be plugged into your listings in your Etsy shop later.

Pinterest Quick Start

Pinterest is an excellent tool to push targeted traffic to your Etsy store. In reality, Pinterest is built to function like a search engine, unlike other social networking sites such as Facebook or Twitter, where people can easily discover new content and then save the content to their own boards.

Moreover, with Pinterest, as other social media posts frequently do, pins do not expire or vanish in a sea of posts. That means they are still available and at any moment, even months later, can end up going viral!

The organic reach that you'll get from Pinterest is also far superior to that of Instagram, Twitter or Facebook.

When it comes to creating an audience on Pinterest, the most important thing is that you spend time each day collecting new material.

In fact, reliability is always the one thing that is lacking from those who fail to create a successful company.

In constantly focusing on raising visibility and building a loyal client base, you want to be vigilant. Doing this will put you miles ahead of the contest.

It all starts with creating a fully optimized Pinterest account that clearly defines your brand, activates the search engine algorithms by sending signals as to what your business is about, and then siphoning traffic to your shop.

Again, keep in mind that Pinterest is a search engine rather than a traditional social platform like Facebook, so you want to focus on **integrating targeted keywords into your account** wherever possible, such as on all your boards and pins so that you are **maximizing visibility** based on specific search queries.

To get started, if you already have a personal account, you'll want to upgrade to a business account at:

https://pinterest.com/business/convert

This will not only help you develop a professional profile on Pinterest, but it will also give you access to significant knowledge that would otherwise be inaccessible to you.

Next, you will be asked by Pinterest where you would like to start. Tap on "Your Brand Showcase."

You'll want to add a profile picture next. You may want to use an image of yourself if possible, but you can still use your Etsy logo or a mascot representing your company.

The key is to maintain a cohesive theme across all platforms. So, on Instagram, your blog, Etsy, and/or your Facebook business page, whatever company name and profile picture you use on Pinterest should also be included.

In that area, the important thing is to use 2 or more keywords. Again, you can always use your main keyword in the area of your company name.

Example:

Your Printable Business Name: Keyword, Keyword, Keyword

Now it's time to apply for rich pins.

Rich pins are an **upgraded version of regular pins** that can help increase visibility and overall engagement. The rich pin content is pulled from your blog titles and posts, or if pinning from your Etsy shop, the pin will pull content from your product listing title and description.

But the biggest benefit of using rich pins is that a Follow connection will be included in your pins, while pins that do not have rich pins allowed will not.

In addition, rich pins will also have a connection to your main Pinterest profile, unlike standard pins, further encouraging engagement!

Now, you'll need to build one post on your blog before you can trigger Rich Pins. It doesn't matter what the content is, it's only used on the website to check the metadata.

So, on your blog, make a post and save it. At the top of your blog post, copy the URL. In the next step, you'll need it.

Now, you'll need to visit:

https://developers.pinterest.com/tools/url-debugger/

Enter the URL you just copied into the text box (your blog post URL) and click Validate to complete the process.

Now you're ready to to level up your Pinterest marketing game, which means you'll want to sign up for Tailwind here: http://tailwindapp.com/

Nothing beats the strength of Tailwind when it comes to reducing your workload, being consistent and getting the most out of your Pinterest marketing.

TailWind is a robust scheduling tool that will allow you to set up bulk pins at pre-determined times so that they go out automatically.

Not only does it put you in full control of being able to schedule your pins so that you're not spending hours a day updating your

Pinterest account, but this tool will show you the best time of day to post your pins to maximize exposure.

Create your free account to begin with, and then you will be prompted to link your account to Pinterest.

You will also be able to download the Chrome plugin once it's completed, so that Tailwind can go to work in your browser directly.

The in-depth analytics they share with you is one of my favorite things about Tailwind. This helps you to control performance quickly so that you can see how people react to your pins and track your outreach, including the growth of followers.

The better you understand your audience by monitoring what pins are getting more likes and saves, the easier it will be for you to create additional boards that are bound to drive in traffic.

Conclusion

It can be fun and simple, as well as extremely profitable, to develop a company in the printable market. Printables continue to rise in popularity and chances are you'll see printables being used regardless of the industry.

There is an endless market for well-designed printables, from aim settings, time trackers, organizational maps, productivity planners to basic calendars and journal type layouts.

Start by choosing a **specific niche** and create printables that cater to the needs of that particular audience. This is called casting a narrow net rather than a wide one.

For example, you could launch an Etsy shop selling health and fitness planners, specifically targeting those who are looking to track their weight loss progress, or who are focused on a particular diet like low carb or keto.

Then, branch out as you get an idea as to what other types of printables they are most interested in. Plug in a traffic source like Pinterest and focus on just one campaign at a time.

Make sure you optimize your whole store, beginning with the title and description, as well as all product listings. Centered on your focal keyword, inject tags and highlight the advantages of your printables.

Later, by providing discount codes exclusive to your newsletter subscribers, or offering free printables to current customers to create and nurture your relationships while solidifying your brand, you can start building a targeted mailing list.

And above all, work to create your printable inventory at all times. The more items you have in your store, the more cash you make: it's as easy as that. Each new product opens the doors for additional traffic, ranking and optimization for other keywords that individuals use when searching for items such as yours.

Yeah, it'll take work, but the big thing about it is that once you've built a decent-sized inventory on Etsy, without having to do as much as you do when you're just starting out, you're going to be able to update regularly.

Stocking those shelves is critical!

Instead of only offering them a few choices, you want customers to be able to visit your shop and have plenty to choose from, so spend some time loading up your store before you concentrate on marketing tactics.

Goal: Aim for 50 listings minimum, 100 listings even better.

Plus, Etsy rewards shops that consistently update with fresh offers so work on a simple content schedule that keeps your storefront loaded with new products every week or month. You'll notice the increase in exposure and of course, the increase in sales every time you update!

And finally, download the Etsy app so you can keep track of sales and communicate with buyers. It's a great way to stay on top of your store and respond to inquiries or support requests.

To your success!

Resources

Here are links to a few resources that I believe will help you:

MarmaLead:

>> https://www.MarmaLead.com

Done-For-You Printables with Commerical-Use Rights:

>> https://shop.nicheraiders.com

Design Etsy Shop Graphics Easily:

>> https://www.Canva.com

TailWind (Pinterest Traffic Tool):

>> http://tailwindapp.com

Made in the USA
Las Vegas, NV
27 August 2022

54113973R00020